Usborne English
Level 2

The Firebird

Retold by Mairi Mackinnon

Illustrated by Sara Ugolotti

English language consultant: Peter Viney

Contents

≪≪≪

You can listen to the story online here:
usborne.com/firebirdaudio

There was once a rich and powerful king, and he had three sons. The king lived in a beautiful palace, and beside the palace was a wonderful garden. The trees in the garden were gold and silver, and their flowers and fruit were shining jewels.

The king liked to walk in the garden every morning, sometimes with his sons or his servants, and sometimes alone.

One September morning, his servants heard a shout. They found the king beside an apple tree in the middle of the garden. This was no ordinary tree. The apples were golden apples – and one was missing.

"Look!" The king pointed at the tree. "Someone has stolen an apple!"

"Impossible, sir!" the servants said. There was a high wall around the garden, and the gates were always locked. That night, guards stood outside the gates and around the walls – but the next day, another apple was missing.

"We didn't see anything," the guards told the king.

"Perhaps they were asleep," said Dimitri, the king's son. "Father, let me watch with them tonight."

He brought more guards. It was a long, cold night. Prince Dimitri tried not to think about his warm, comfortable bed.

Morning came… and another apple was missing.

"We didn't see anybody," Dimitri told his father. The next night his brother, Prince Vassily, watched with the guards, and the same thing happened.

"Father, let me watch tonight," said Ivan, the youngest prince.

His brothers laughed. "What can you do? You're only a boy. This isn't an ordinary thief, you know. An ordinary thief couldn't climb over the wall or through the locked gates. This must be a powerful sorcerer!"

Prince Ivan waited under the apple tree. It was very cold, and the stars were very bright.

The prince walked up and down to stay warm, and sang songs to stay awake.

Towards morning, he saw light in the sky. "Is that the sun already?" he wondered.

The light came closer. Ivan saw a beautiful bird with wings of fire and a long, bright tail. The bird flew around the garden and down to the apple tree. It opened its beak to take an apple. Ivan jumped up and tried to catch it, but its body was burning hot. It flew away, and all he had was one red-gold feather from its tail.

The king was amazed. "So our thief is a Firebird. How wonderful! A Firebird in my garden!"

Prince Dimitri said, "Sir, you must have this lovely bird in your garden always."

"I'd like that," said the king.

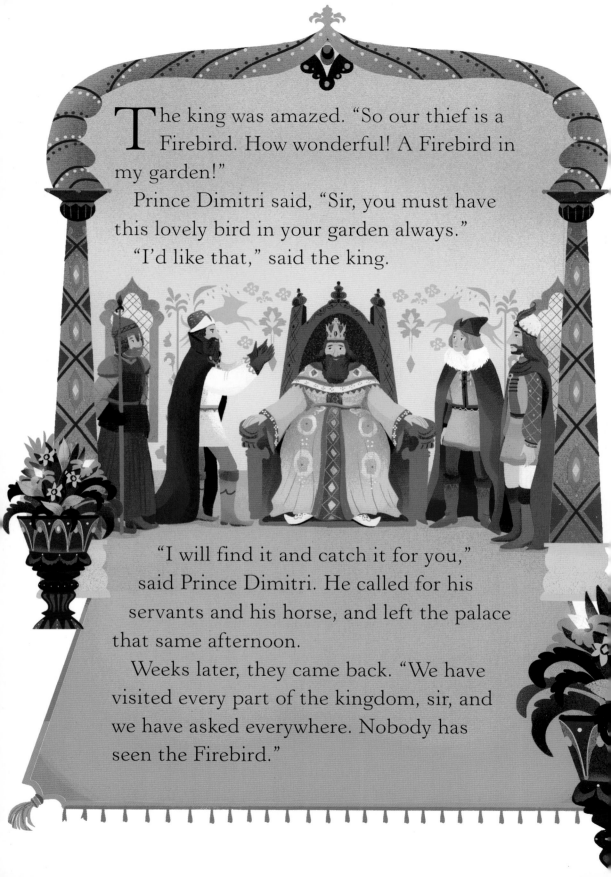

"I will find it and catch it for you," said Prince Dimitri. He called for his servants and his horse, and left the palace that same afternoon.

Weeks later, they came back. "We have visited every part of the kingdom, sir, and we have asked everywhere. Nobody has seen the Firebird."

Prince Vassily said, "Let me try." Weeks later, he too came back. "We went to every town and city, and even searched outside the kingdom. I'm sorry, sir. The Firebird is just a story for children."

Prince Ivan said, "But I saw it, and I showed you its red-gold feather. Believe me, sir, I will find it for you."

"What, now – in the middle of winter?" Dimitry and Vassily laughed. "Stay at home, little brother. No servant will travel with you at this time of year."

"Then I'll go alone," said Prince Ivan. He put on his warm winter cloak, and took the Firebird's feather with him. Then he rode out from the palace.

Soon he was riding through an enormous forest. There was snow all around him. There were no animals or birds, and Ivan could hear no other sounds. He saw a signpost, and stopped and read it:

YOU WILL DIE HERE

WOLVES WILL EAT YOU

GO BACK

YOU WILL FAIL

"I'm not afraid of wolves," said Ivan loudly. Suddenly a huge silver wolf jumped out from the trees and attacked his horse. Ivan fell to the ground.

"I'm sorry," the wolf said. "I couldn't stop myself." He was looking into Ivan's eyes.

"You've killed my horse," said Ivan. "Are you going to kill me?"

"Oh, I don't think so," said the wolf. "Maybe I can help you instead."

"*You* – help *me*?" asked Ivan. "I have to find the Firebird for my father. My two brothers have failed already, and now I don't even have a horse to ride."

"Well, you can ride on my back," said the wolf. "I will carry you to King Dalmat's palace. You'll find the Firebird there."

Ivan climbed carefully onto the animal's back. He was amazed when Silver Wolf jumped high into the air, up above the treetops. They flew over the forest, above snowy fields and icy rivers. The moon and stars were bright in the sky above them. Then they saw the lights of a city below them, and the gardens of another palace.

Silver Wolf came down under some tall trees.

"Do you see that tower?" he said to Ivan. "The Firebird is in a room at the top of the tower."

"The door isn't locked, and nobody will stop you. Go and take the Firebird – but don't touch her cage."

Prince Ivan climbed the stairs and opened the door to the tower room. There was the Firebird, as bright as the sun. "How can I carry her without a cage, though?" thought Ivan. "She'll burn me if I even touch her."

He picked up the cage, and immediately he heard loud bells all through the palace. Guards hurried into the room and dragged the prince away.

The next morning, they took him to King Dalmat.

"How can a prince like you be a thief?" asked the king.

"Sir, let me explain," said Ivan. He told the king the story of the Firebird and his father's garden.

"Hmm. Shall I give you the Firebird?" asked the king. "Well, you can have her, but you must do one thing for me. Many years ago, King Saltan stole my Horse of Power. Bring her back to me, and the Firebird will be yours."

"You can keep that feather," the king added. "Some day, it may help you."

Prince Ivan went to find Silver Wolf, and
soon they were flying through the air again,
over the mountains and across the sea.
     In the evening they saw the lights of
another city and another palace. Silver
Wolf came down in the palace gardens.

"Do you see the stables?" he said to Ivan.
"The Horse of Power is there, at the farthest
end. The doors aren't locked, and nobody
will stop you. You can bring her out —
but don't touch her bridle."

Quietly, Ivan opened the stable door.
There was the Horse of Power, a
beautiful golden animal with silver wings.
He reached out with his hand, and she
moved away.

"I will need a bridle," he thought.
"I suppose that's her bridle, with the
jewels — but surely I can take this
other one."

Immediately, he heard bells all the way
to the palace. Guards hurried into the
stables and dragged the prince away.

The next morning, they took him
to King Saltan.

"Why does a prince like you want to steal horses?" asked the king.

"Sir, let me explain," said Ivan. He told the king the story of the Firebird, Silver Wolf and King Dalmat. "Is there something I can do for you, sir?" he added.

"There is one thing," King Saltan said slowly.

He showed Ivan a picture. "This is my daughter, the princess Marya. Many years ago, the sorcerer Kaschey stole her when she was playing with her friends in the palace gardens."

"I haven't seen her since that day, but I know she is still alive," said the king. "Our bravest knights and princes went to search for her. They never came back."

"I will find her, sir," said Ivan.

"Do you know what you are saying? Kaschey is very old and very powerful and very wicked. They call him Kaschey the Deathless. So many have failed before you, young man. I hope you will not fail."

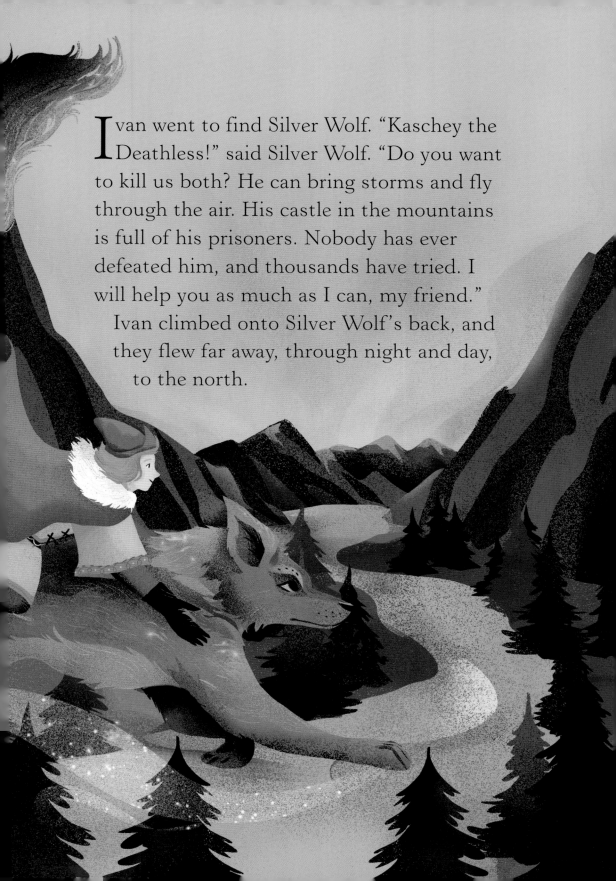

Ivan went to find Silver Wolf. "Kaschey the Deathless!" said Silver Wolf. "Do you want to kill us both? He can bring storms and fly through the air. His castle in the mountains is full of his prisoners. Nobody has ever defeated him, and thousands have tried. I will help you as much as I can, my friend."

Ivan climbed onto Silver Wolf's back, and they flew far away, through night and day, to the north.

Finally they saw a dark stone castle in the snow and ice of the high mountains. Silver Wolf came down to the ground, a little way from the castle. "We'll wait until it is dark," he said. "You may be lucky. Kaschey will not expect you."

When the moon came up over the mountains, Ivan climbed onto Silver Wolf's back again, and the wolf jumped high into the air. Inside the castle walls, Ivan was surprised to see a garden full of trees, flowers and statues.

Silver Wolf came down in a corner of the garden, and Ivan started walking towards the castle. Then he heard music and voices between the trees.

Twelve pretty girls were dancing in the moonlight. "Marya, won't you join us?" one asked, and a thirteenth girl appeared, more beautiful than all the others.

She was older than in the king's picture, but Ivan recognized her immediately. He ran forward. "Princess, don't be frightened. Silver Wolf and I have come to take you home to your father. You are safe with us."

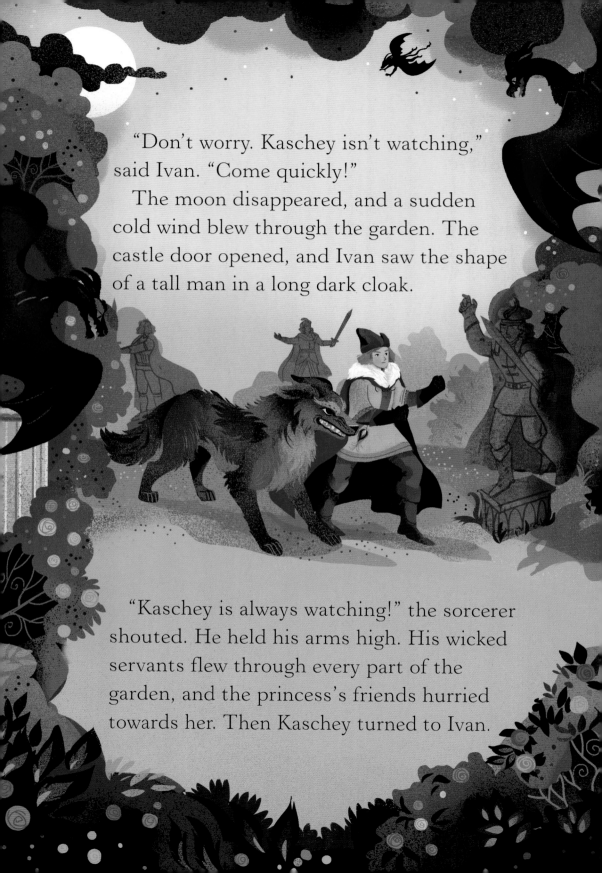

"Don't worry. Kaschey isn't watching," said Ivan. "Come quickly!"

The moon disappeared, and a sudden cold wind blew through the garden. The castle door opened, and Ivan saw the shape of a tall man in a long dark cloak.

"Kaschey is always watching!" the sorcerer shouted. He held his arms high. His wicked servants flew through every part of the garden, and the princess's friends hurried towards her. Then Kaschey turned to Ivan.

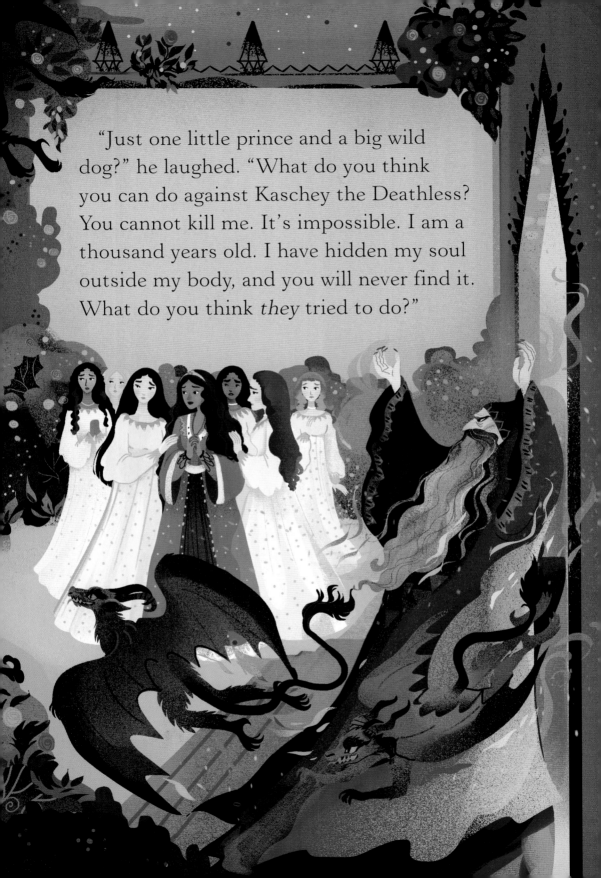

"Just one little prince and a big wild dog?" he laughed. "What do you think you can do against Kaschey the Deathless? You cannot kill me. It's impossible. I am a thousand years old. I have hidden my soul outside my body, and you will never find it. What do you think *they* tried to do?"

He pointed to the statues, and Ivan
looked more closely. He saw the stone
knights and princes with their swords held
high, and he understood.

"Too late, little prince!" Kaschey laughed.
"It's time for you to join them!"

Ivan couldn't feel his feet or his
legs. He looked down and saw that
they were turning to stone.

The castle door closed and the wind stopped. Something fell to Ivan's feet. It was the Firebird's feather! Soon his body felt alive and warm again.

"Quickly, Ivan!" said Silver Wolf. "Go to the dead tree, there in the corner. Find the box inside it, and inside that you'll find the sorcerer's soul. You'll know what to do." Ivan ran to the tree. He reached inside it and pulled out a dark metal box. He opened the box and took out a golden egg.

"NOOOO!!" Kaschey screamed from the castle door. "Give it to me! I'll give you anything you want!"

Ivan threw the egg from one hand to the other, and Kaschey flew through the air. Then Ivan threw the egg on the ground, and it broke into a thousand pieces. The sky turned black and the castle walls shook.

"Wake up, Ivan." It was Silver Wolf's voice. Ivan opened his eyes. The garden was full of sunshine, and he couldn't see the castle at all.

There was the princess and there were her friends, laughing and crying together. There were other voices, too. Ivan saw the knights and princes. They were touching their living faces and stretching their arms and legs.

Princess Marya was beside him. "Thank you, Ivan," she said.

"Thank you," said her friends, and the knights and princes.

"Thank you," said hundreds more voices, men and women together. "We have been Kaschey's prisoners for hundreds of years. We never expected to see the light again."

"Thank you," said thousands more. "Before Kaschey built his castle, this was our city. Thank you for saving us!"

The next day, Ivan and the princess said goodbye and climbed onto Silver Wolf's back. Soon they were high in the air, flying south to King Saltan's palace, and soon Marya and her father were together again. The king held his daughter close. He was crying with happiness. "How can I thank you enough?" he asked Ivan.

"Please, stay here with us," said Marya. "I'd like that," said Ivan, "but first I must take the Horse of Power to King Dalmat, and I must take the Firebird to my father."

"Then let us come with you," said the King. He rode the Horse of Power, and Ivan and the princess rode Silver Wolf through the sky to King Dalmat's palace.

There, the two kings shook hands like brothers. Servants took the Horse of Power into King Dalmat's stables, and brought the Firebird in her cage to Prince Ivan.

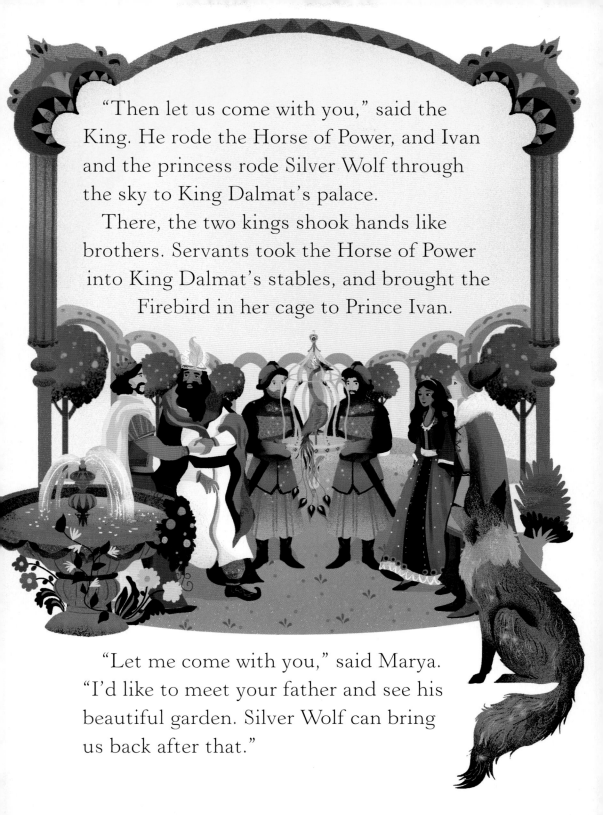

"Let me come with you," said Marya. "I'd like to meet your father and see his beautiful garden. Silver Wolf can bring us back after that."

Ivan's father was sitting alone in his garden. His face was full of sadness and his clothes were heavy black. When Silver Wolf came down beside the apple tree, the king couldn't believe it. He jumped up and ran forward.

"Ivan! You're alive!"

Ivan opened the cage. The Firebird stretched her wings, flew around the garden and took an apple in her long beak.

Then she flew down to where the king was standing.

"How wonderful!" the king said.

"I won't keep her here," he decided.

"She must fly where she wants; but I hope she will come back often."

"Father, this is the princess Marya," said Ivan, "and this is my friend Silver Wolf, who attacked my horse and saved my life…"

"…and who brought Ivan to my father's palace and to Koschey's castle, where he defeated the sorcerer and saved us all," added the princess.

"And all thanks to this beautiful apple thief," said the king with a smile.

About the story

The Firebird is one of the best-known and best-loved stories in Russia. There are often pictures of the Firebird and other characters from the story on the painted wooden boxes that are very popular in Russia. (You can see one here on the left.)

Russia has many fairy tales and legends. They are not always so well known in the rest of the world. Several include the character of Prince Ivan, the youngest son of a king. Nobody expects much from the young prince, but he often has magical helpers.

As well as stories and paintings, the Firebird inspired a famous ballet in 1910, with music by Igor Stravinsky. The ballet is still popular around the world today. On the right you can see dancers in the characters of the Firebird and the Prince.

Activities

The answers are on page 40.

Who's who?

Choose *two* sentences for each character.

The Firebird   Prince Ivan   Princess Marya   Kaschey

A. …catches a feather from the Firebird's tail.	**B.** …takes an apple in her long beak.
C. …was stolen from the palace gardens by the sorcerer.	**D.** …is always watching.
E. …promises that he will find the princess.	**F.** …has hidden his soul outside his body.
G. … is more beautiful than all the other girls.	**H.** …can fly where she wants.

Mixed-up story

Can you put these pictures and sentences in order?

A.

Ivan was surprised to see a garden full of flowers and statues.

B.

Ivan jumped up and tried to catch the bird.

C.

The King liked to walk in the garden every morning.

D.

"I will carry you to King Dalmat's palace," said the silver wolf.

E.

"How can a prince like you be a thief?" asked the king.

F.

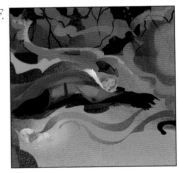

The egg broke into a thousand pieces.

G.

"What do you think you can do against Kaschey the Deathless?"

H.

"Look! Someone has stolen an apple!"

I.

"Is there something I can do for you, sir?" Ivan added.

Who says this?

Match the words to the right person.

Prince Vassily

King Saltan

Princess Marya

Ivan's father

A. "Please, stay here with us."

B. "The Firebird is just a story for children."

C. "I hope she will come back often."

D. "I know she is still alive."

What happened next?

Choose the right sentence.

1.

Prince Dimitri watched the apple tree with the guards.

A. He caught the Firebird's tail feather.

B. In the morning, another apple was missing.

2.

Ivan saw a signpost in the forest.

A. Silver Wolf attacked his horse.

B. He decided to go back to the palace.

3.

Ivan reached for the plain bridle.

A. He led the Horse of Power out of the stable.

B. He heard bells all the way to the palace.

4.

Silver Wolf came down in a corner of the garden.

A. Ivan saw the shape of a man in a long dark cloak.

B. Ivan heard music and voices between the trees.

Is that right?

One word in each sentence is wrong.
Can you find it and choose the right word instead?

1.

"Sir, you must have this lovely bird in your palace always."

stables   tower   garden

2.

He was asleep when Silver Wolf flew high into the air.

amazed   afraid   alive

3.

"Too late, little prince!" Kaschey thought.

added   heard   laughed

4.

"We have been Kaschey's guards for hundreds of years."

servants   prisoners   brothers

Word list

attack (v) if you attack someone, you start a fight and try to hurt or even kill them.

beak (n) a bird's mouth and nose are in its beak.

bell (n) bells are usually made of metal and make a musical sound.

bridle (n) the harness around a horse's head and neck that helps you to lead it or ride it.

cage (n) a container made of wood or metal. You keep an animal or a bird in a cage so that it can't run or fly away.

cloak (n) a kind of long coat without sleeves.

defeat (v) when you defeat someone, you win a fight or a competition against them.

drag (v) when you drag something, you pull it hard along the ground.

fail (v) when you are unable to do something you want to do or try to do, you fail.

feather (n) birds have feathers on their bodies and their wings. Their feathers help them to fly.

guard (n) someone who keeps a person or a place safe.

jewel (n) a precious stone. For example, a diamond is a jewel.

kingdom (n) a country that has a king.

knight (n) a man who serves the king or a lord, and will go and fight for him.

locked (adj) when something is locked, you can only open it with a key.

power (n) strength or being able to do something.

powerful (adj) having power; strong.

prisoner (n) someone who is in a prison and is not free.

search (v) to look very carefully for someone or something.

servant (n) someone who works for another person, especially in their home.

shake, shook (v) when something shakes, it moves quickly from side to side. You might shake hands to say hello to a person by holding and moving their hand up and down.

signpost (n) signposts are usually made of wood or metal, and you might see one beside a road, telling you which way to go.

sorcerer (n) a magician, usually an evil one.

soul (n) the part of your mind that believes things, dreams and feels emotions.

stable (n) a place for keeping horses.

statue (n) a model of a person, made of stone or metal. Statues are usually life size or larger.

stretch (v) when you make something reach as far as you can, you stretch it. You might stretch your arms to help you wake up.

thief, thieves (n) someone who steals things.

tower (n) a very tall building or part of a building.

wolf, wolves (n) a large wild dog that lives in mountains and forests.

Answers

Who's who?
The Firebird – B, H
Prince Ivan – A, E
Princess Marya – C, G
Kaschey – D, F

Mixed-up story
C, H, B, D, E,
I, A, G, F

Who says this?
Prince Vassily – B
King Saltan – D
Princess Marya – A
Ivan's father – C

What happened next?
1. B
2. A
3. B
4. B

Is that right?
1. ~~palace~~ garden
2. ~~asleep~~ amazed
3. ~~thought~~ laughed
4. ~~guards~~ prisoners

You can find information about
other Usborne English Readers here:
usborne.com/englishreaders

Designed by Jodie Smith
Series designer: Laura Nelson Norris
Edited by Jane Chisholm

Page 32: Jewel box 'The Firebird' © Sputnik / TopFoto
Photo from The Royal Ballet, 'The Firebird' © Dee Conway / Bridgeman Images

First published in 2021 by Usborne Publishing Ltd.,
Usborne House, 83-85 Saffron Hill, London EC1N 8RT, England.
usborne.com Copyright © 2021 Usborne Publishing Ltd.